'GULLY' by Jon Cleave
FANCY A TAKE-AWAY, DEAR?
THAT'D BE NICE - WHAT IS THERE?
GULLY AND THE PRINCESS DISCUSS THEIR DINING ARRANGEMENTS...
WELL, THERE'S FISH & CHIPS, ICE CREAM, CANDY FLOSS, BURGERS, PASTIES, NUGGETS...
FRED'S
BURGERS
ICES
FISH'N'CHIPS
TAKE
www.thegullery.co.uk

'GULLY' by Jon Claxwell
SUNDAY SPORT WITH THE GULLYS
READY YET?
NO, NOT QUITE
SPARKLE
NOW?
YEP, I SHOULD THINK SO!
COME ON PRINCESS - BOMBS AWAY!
GLEAM
www.thegullery.co.uk

'GULLY' by Jon Cleave
YEUCH!!
GULLY IS A LITTLE BIT FUSSY...
UGH!!
YOU CAN'T BEAT A PROPER CORNISH PASTY, CAN YOU?
www.thegullery.co.uk

'GULLY' by JON CLEAVE
YOU WERE LATE BACK LAST NIGHT GULLY
NOT THAT LATE PRINCESS
HOW MANY DID YOU HAVE?
ONLY A COUPLE LUV
RUBBISH! I BET YOU HAD AT LEAST 3. YOU HAD 3, DIDN'T YOU?
I CAN HARDLY REMEMBER. WAS IT 6? NO, IT WAS 7..
OH ALL RIGHT, 3 THEN. YOU KNOW ME TOO WELL, PRINCESS.
HOW CAN YOU FLY HOME WITH 3 PASTIES INSIDE YOU?
www.thegullery.co.uk

'GULLY' by JON CLEAVE
PRINCESS, WE'VE BEEN TOGETHER 25 YEARS, AND IT DON'T SEEM A DAY TOO LONG.
OH, GULLY
GULLY IS GETTING ALL LOVEY DOVEY
I MEAN IT PRINCESS, YOU'RE THE MOST BEAUTIFUL GULL IN THE WORLD...
OH GULLY, THAT'S SO NICE
♫ IF I WAS THE ONLY BOY IN THE WORLD, ♩ AND YOU WERE THE ONLY GULL ♫
GULLY, YOU SAY THE NICEST THINGS
GO GET US A PASTY THEN, LUV.
THINK I'D FALL FOR THAT? GO GET YOUR OWN!

'GULLY' by JON CLEAVE
SO, YOU'RE NEW TO THE VILLAGE? WELL I HOPE YOU SETTLE IN OK.
THANK YOU GULLY.
THERE'S A NEWCOMER IN TOWN
I THINK YOU'LL FIND US A FRIENDLY BUNCH HERE...
I'M SURE I WILL
WHERE DID YOU SAY YOU WERE FROM?
NEWQU....
WHAT DID I SAY?

'GULLY' by JON CLEAVE
I CAN READ YOUR MIND, GULLY. I CAN TELL WHAT YOU'RE THINKING
THE PRINCESS IS STUDYING GULLY
I KNOW YOU SO WELL
YOU DON'T GIVE A S--T, DO YOU?
WELL THAT'S JUST WHERE YOU'RE WRONG PRINCESS!
I'M JUST ABOUT TO

'GULLY' by Jon Cleave
FISH A LITTLE OVERDONE, CHIPS FRANKLY LIKE CARDBOARD. BUT, OVERALL, QUITE REASONABLE FOR THE LOWER END OF THE MARKET.
THE GREASY SPOON
GULLY IS EATING OUT
SIRLOIN & CHIPS, BLACK FOREST GATEAU, PRAWN COCKTAIL....OH MY NOSTALGIC TASTE BUDS!
BUT THE BLUE NUN — WHAT A NASTY HABIT THAT WAS!
SEVENTIES HEAVEN
BL N
SO, LET'S SEE IF THIS IS ALL IT'S CRACKED UP TO BE, SHALL WE?
OK, I THINK I'LL START WITH...
STEIN'S SEAFOOD RESTAU
www.thegullery.co.uk

'GULLY' by JON CLEAVE
SEE PRINCESS, THE POTATO IS SLICED, NOT DICED, AND WE USE SKIRT BEEF, AND PLENTY OF SEASONING....
OH, I SEE
THE HISTORY OF THE PASTY
AND THAT BIT YOU'RE EATING NOW - THAT'S THE CRIMPING. IT USED TO STOP TIN MINERS GETTING ARSENIC FROM THEIR FINGERS INTO THEIR MOUTHS..
REALLY? HOW FASCINATING.
THANK YOU GULLY, THAT WAS SO INTERESTING...
MY PLEASURE
... AND DELICIOUS
I CAN SEE THAT!

'GULLY' by JON CLEAVE!
♫ THE OTHER NIGHT I HAD A DREAM, THE FUNNIEST DREAM OF ALL ♩♩
GULLY IS SINGING TO THE PRINCESS
♩♩ I DREAMT THAT I WAS KISSING YOU, ♩♩ BEHIND THE GARDEN WALL ♫ ♩
OH NO YOU DON'T MATEY!
REMEMBER WHAT HAPPENED LAST TIME?
NO...
WELL I DO!

'GULLY' by JON CLEAVE
HERE YOU GO GUYS. A NICE MACKEREL SKELETON.
IT'S CHICK FEEDING TIME...
AND A NICE PASTY
AND SOME NUGGETS AND CHIPS
AND A LOVELY ICE CREAM.
YOU'RE SPOILING THEM GULLY. THEY HAVEN'T EATEN THEIR SAVOURY YET.

'GULLY' by JON CLEAVE
GIVE IT BACK!
Oi!
ITS THE GULYMPICS
HERE, THATS MY PASTY!
CONGRATULATIONS YOU WON!
ST. IVES
PADSTOW
THANK YOU
IT SHOULD HAVE BEEN ME!
PORT ISAAC
GOLD
SILVER
BRONZE

'GULLY' by Jon Cleave
OH ARR, OH ARR, I AM A CIDER DRINKER...
WHAT'S HE SAYING GULLY?
I CAN'T MAKE IT OUT...
//GULLY HEARS AN ODD DIALECT
OI GOT A BRAND NEW COMBINE HARVESTER OH ARR, OH ARR
IT'S NOT CORNISH, IS IT?
NO, IT'S DEFINITELY NOT CORNISH - NOT AS WE KNOW IT...
OH ARR, OH ARRRR!.... IT'S BOOTIFULL, REALLY BOOTIFULL... GET ORF MOI LAND... I LUV MISS DIANE, I DO...
MAYBE HE'S A LUNATIC?
PRINCESS, I FEAR IT'S WORSE THAN THAT. I'M AFRAID HE'S FROM THE DOC MARTIN CAST!
www.thegullery.co.uk

'GULLY' by Jon Cleave
LOOK AT ALL THE FASHIONS, GULLY. WHAT'S *IN* THIS YEAR, I WONDER?
CORNWALL IS SO TRENDY NOW...
STRIPES, FLORAL, CHECKED, PLAIN? BRIGHT, PASTEL, MUTED? FUTURISTIC, RETRO? I REALLY DON'T KNOW....
I DO. IT'S POLKA-DOT AGAIN
HOW DO YOU KNOW THAT, GULLY?
JUST WATCH & LEARN, PRINCESS. WATCH & LEARN!
www.thegullery.co.uk

'GULLY' by JON CLEAVE
DICK SWINE'S
SO, THE SKATE DARLING?
PERFECT.
I SAY, EXCUSE ME. I HOPE YOU DON'T MIND..
GILES AND ARABELLA ARE DINING OUT AT SWINE'S
DICK SWINE'S
REALLY? I SAY, THANKS AWFULLY
IT'S JUST THAT THE BONES ARE RATHER FIDDLY ON THE SKATE
DICK SWINE'S
WHAT WAS THAT, DARLING?
JUST ONE OF THE LOCALS, ADVISING AGAINST THE SKATE
HOW SWEET!
I LIKE TO BE HELPFUL - SOMETIMES

'GULLY' by JON CLEAVE
EENY, MEENY, MINY, MO, SPOT A TAKE-AWAY BELOW,
GULLY IS FEELING POETIC
FISH, CHIPS & PASTIES, ALL TO GO
EENY, MEENY, MINY
MO!

'GULLY' by Jon Cleave
FOLLOW THE PLOUGH?
THE TRADITIONAL FEEDING GROUNDS
FOLLOW THE TRAWLER?
TAKE AWAY
NAAA!
ANYTHING FOR AN EASY LIFE!
www.thegullery.co.uk

'GULLY' by JON CLEAVE
IT MUST BE A HONEY BUZZARD
OR A BEWICK'S SWAN
WHAT ABOUT A LITTLE EGRET
THE TWITCHERS ARE OUT - AGAIN
RELAX MY FRIENDS. THAT IS JUST AN ORDINARY, COMMON & GARDEN, RUN OF THE MILL HERRING GULL
ORDINARY? COMMON! GARDEN? RUN OF THE MILL!
HAVE YOU EVER SEEN A GREATER SPOTTED TWITCHER?

'GULLY' by JON CLEAVE
MEDALLIONS OF MONKFISH, CREVETTES, JACKET POTATO, BUTTON MUSHROOMS...
DICK SWINE'S RESTAU
MENU
THERE'S A NEW MENU AT SWINES'
... IN A CHOUX PASTRY. HA! CAN'T SPELL, EH? EVERYONE KNOWS IT'S SHOE!
DICK SWINE'S RESTAU
MENU
ANYWAY, WHAT DO YOU DO WITH THIS? EAT IT OR WEAR IT?
DICK SWINE'S RESTAURANT
MENU

'GULLY' by Jon Cleave
GULLY, THIS IS ME NEW GULLFRIEND.
GULLY'S MATE IS COURTING STRONG
VERY NICE. WHERE'S HER FROM?
PADSTOW
WELL, HER SEEMS LIKE A PROPER OLD MAID.
OLD MAID? CHEEKY DEVIL!
WWW.thegullery.co.uk

'GULLY' by JON CLEAVE
YOU CAN GO DOWN AND PLAY ON THE BEACH, LIKE I USED TO. THERE'S ALWAYS LOTS OF FOOD DOWN THERE.
GULLY IS PARENTING
THEN, WHEN YOU'VE LEARNED TO FLY, YOU CAN FOLLOW THE FISHING BOATS OUT TO SEA, OR FLY INLAND TO FORAGE ON THE FIELDS OR AT THE DUMP, OR HANG OUT AT THE TAKE AWAY, OR AT RICK STEIN'S..
THERE'S NEVER BEEN A BETTER TIME TO BE A GULL!

'GULLY' By Jon Cleave!
GULLY, WE COULD DO WITH SOME MORE SEAWEED IN THE NEST, & SOME TWIGS & STUFF, & MAYBE YOU COULD TIDY UP SOME FISH BONES....
ZZZZZ
GULLY IS TAKING A NAP....
....AND GET RID OF THAT OLD CRISP BAG, AND THOSE OLD BITS OF CRAB SHELL...
YEA, ALL RIGHT DEAR
DRECKLY, EH?
ZZZZZ
www.thegullery.co.uk

'GULLY' by JON CLEAVE
SO, LADIES AND GENTLEMEN, TODAY WE CAN EXPECT TO SEE MANY WONDERS OF MOTHER NATURE.
AA
GANNET DIVING FOR FISH, MAYBE DOLPHIN...
THE NATURE GUIDE IS OUT
ATLANTIC & GREY SEAL, BASKING SHARK, PEREGRINE FALCON STOOPING ON THEIR PREY..
Oi!
AREN'T YOU GOING TO TELL THEM ABOUT THE MOST HANDSOME & INTELLIGENT & SUCCESSFUL SEABIRD THEN?

'GULLY' by Jon Cleave
WHO ARE THEY, GULLY?
THAT'S HUGO AND JACASTA.
GULLY AND THE PRINCESS HAVE GOT NEW NEIGHBOURS
WHERE ARE THEY FROM? CAMBOURNE?
NO, PRINCESS. THEY'RE DOWN FROM LONDON FOR THE WEEKEND
THEY'VE COME DOWN TO THEIR SECOND NEST.
SHOULDN'T BE ALLOWED...
NOW, NOW, PRINCESS. THEY ARE TERRIBLY NICE.

'GULLY' by JON CLEAVE
IT'S A NICE NEW ICE CREAM PARLOUR, ISN'T IT GULLY?
YES, PROPER JOB.
ICES
ISH ICE CREAM
A NEW SHOP HAS OPENED
LOOK AT THAT. VANILLA, STRAWBERRY, CHOCOLATE, RASPBERRY RIPPLE...
ICES
ISH ICE CREAM
CRUSHED NUTS, CHOCO SAUCE, MAPLE SYRUP...
ICES
ISH ICECREAM
I REALLY CAN'T MAKE MY MIND UP!
www.thegullery.co.uk

'GULLY' by JON CLEAVE
POOR DIGORY. HIM & HIS MISSUS HAVE 4 CHICKS EVERY YEAR
GULLY IS VISITING HIS MATE DIGORY
THEY'VE ONLY GOT 2 BEAKS LIKE THE REST OF US
BETWEEN YOU & ME, I DON'T KNOW HOW THEY DO IT!

'GULLY' by JON CLEAVE
GOUJONS OF WILD SALMON PRESENTED ON A COMFY BED OF MASH, SUFFUSED WITH THE MEREST HINT, NAY....
DICK SWI MENU
... SUGGESTION OF FENNEL FRONDS, DELICATELY DRIZZLED WITH A FIRST PRESSE, EXTRA VIRGINE OLIVE OIL, SOURCED FROM THE SUN KISSED FOOTHILLS OF SOUTHERN CALABRIA
SO WHAT'S HE AFTER THEN?
A MICHELIN STAR, OR THE BOOKER PRIZE?
G

'GULLY' by JON CLEAVE
THERE! IT'S A GYR FALCON! I TELL YOU - MY FIRST!
ARE YOU SURE?
I'M CERTAIN IT'S AN IMMATURE SKUA...
NO, NO, IT CAN'T BE. IT WOULD BE OFF ICELAND THIS TIME OF THE YEAR
THE TWITCHERS ARE IN TOWN
STAND BACK, ALL OF YOU. THESE BINOCULARS COST OVER A THOUSAND POUNDS, AND THAT LITTLE BEAUTY, MY FRIENDS, IS THE EXTRAORDINARILY RARE LESSER SPOTTED MANX SHEARWATER
OVER A THOUSAND? THEY MUST HAVE SEEN YOU COMING, MATEY!

'GULLY' by JON CLEAVE
SO, WHAT ARE HUGO AND JACASTA UP TO THEN?
DOING UP THEIR SECOND NEST AGAIN.
THE WEEKENDERS ARE DOWN
I DOUBT THEY'VE GOT PLANNING PERMISSION. THEIR SORT NEVER DO, AND I BET THEY GET AWAY WITH IT!
IT LOOKS DREADFULL. NOT AT ALL IN KEEPING. ABSOLUTELY AWFUL!
Hi, GULLY, Hi PRINCESS. SO, WHAT DO YOU THINK, EH?
OH, Hi HUGO. WE WONDERED IF IT WAS YOU. YES, IT LOOKS SIMPLY STUNNING
PERFECT HUGO. COULDN'T BE BETTER
www.thegullery.co.uk

'GULLY' by JON CLEAVE
WHAT'S THE MATTER, GULLY?
IT'S THAT TIME OF YEAR PRINCESS. IT'S GONE SO QUIET
IT'S EARLY NOVEMBER
NO ONE TO DIVE BOMB OR TO SPLAT ON, NO PASTIES OR ICE CREAM TO PINCH. IT'S A GHOST TOWN. THEY'VE ALL GONE HOME. IT'S SO DEPRESSING
SO WHERE ARE YOU OFF TO NOW, EH?
UP TO THE BINS AT THE BACK OF THE SURGERY TO SEE IF THEY'VE CHUCKED OUT ANY PROZAC!

'GULLY' by Jon Cleave
NOW THEN GULLY, YOU'VE HAD YOUR PASTY & CHIPS, HOW ABOUT A NICE ICE CREAM?
MMMM!
THE PRINCESS IS SPOILING GULLY
FLAKE? CHOCOLATE SAUCE? A CORNET OR WAFER? MAPLE SYRUP? Mr WHIPPY? KELLYS? VANILLA OR RIPPLE.....
SOUNDS GOOD TO ME, PRINCESS.
....RASPBERRY SAUCE? 100's & 1000's? AN EXTRA FLAKE? CHOC CHIPS?
DO YOU WANT CRUSHED NUTS?
WHAT CAN I SAY? IT ALL SEEMED TO BE GOING SO WELL.
www.thegullery.co.uk

'GULLY' by JON CLEAVE
SO WHAT'S GOING ON THEN, GULLY?
THE USUAL MOANS. DOG MESS, LITTER, OVERGROWN HEDGES...
..DOG MESS, GRAFFITTI, JUNK MAIL..
GULLY HAS FOUND THE PARISH NEWSLETTER IN THE BINS
QUEUE BARGING IN THE POST OFFICE, COUNCIL TAX, DOG MESS, SATANIC RITUALS, GYPSIES, DOG MESS, LATE BUSES...
AND?
DID I MENTION DOG MESS?
I THINK SO. ANYTHING ELSE?
OH YES. US!